AFTER YOU, IN LOVE ARREST

This work is a poet's depiction of two people in pursuit of love.
Any resemblance to real persons living is purely coincidental.

After You, In Love Arrest
© 2014 by Mario Gabriel Adame

Print Book Edition:
Library of Congress Catalog Number: 2014916516
Dead Poets Dream Publishing, San Antonio, TX

ISBN: 0692278680   ISBN-13: 978-0692278680

back cover original oil painting "Souls petals"
by Alexei Antonov / written permission obtained
www.antonovart.com

"Hope" is the thing with feathers -
That perches in the soul -
And sings the tune without the words -
And never stops - at all -

- Emily Dickinson

After You, In Love Arrest

A Poetry Collection

Mario Gabriel Adame

CONTENTS

ARREST   **61**

AFTER YOU

When you meet a charming woman that makes you want to change your past, it is relatively a living paradox. You want to go back in time, because you want her to be yours for all-time. You want her more than you ever needed any one else, but on the other side, each girl that came before her has led you to her. Because of prior experiences with those girls, you carry wounds of anger, fear, and established insecurity. However, you learned that it takes two in a relationship. You are as responsible for that agony as the person you chose to be with. Do not get me wrong, I have been blessed with a tremendous amount of thrilling, happy, and peaceful moments, time and time again in my past, but the arrest in those relationships has left confusion, isolation, a necessary faith, and the determine search for a cure.

Naturally in a heartbeat you would trade the good and the bad moments of your past to start new with this woman. Your faith runs that deep, as deep as the past in order to live in the present with her and remain open to finding a matrimonial future, together with her as one. Throughout the trade, there is one keynote that is yet to be written, and that key to a language in your heart lies in a question, do you trust yourself to welcome the present and a future, while properly learning from the past and leaving it behind you in order to invite undying moments for finding answers to what it means exactly to be *in love*, and most importantly, to know solutions for staying *in love*?

This is every piece of one thoughtful question, the constant idea you are having at the beginning as you are talking to her and staring at every millimeter of the beautiful brown in her irises. Whether you physically see her in person, in a picture, or on a video chat date, the conversation runs deeper than she knows. This is the chance at a new and final beginning, a beginning you want her to have complete power in possessing the cure. She does not know but you believe in her, you believe she has the perfecting cure of eternal love. Your instinct, unlike ever before, is she has everything it takes. In this world of chaotic technology and instant communication, you have fallen and you are still falling for her because of the calmness, ambitious and sweet tone in her voice on the phone when you cannot see her face. You imagine her eyes, the way her lips are moving, and you wonder what she is daydreaming in return. You have fallen for her because when you see her on a video chat screen and in a picture, or hearing her voice over phone, you imagine her right beside you with her electric touch and genuine body gestures. This is a sweet fantasy but yet real. This is something you never experienced but always wanted and quite frankly need. You listen carefully, and you respect everything she has to say because she has chosen to end her day with you. She has elected to focus on you, to share with you her life in moments, and to welcome your attentive energy.

Keep in mind this embodiment is occurring within the first couple weeks of her sharing that she has had a crush on you since the first time she met you, four years ago. When learning that a mutual crush has always existed throughout time, she says, "Are we really doing this?!" and words like she is "all in." She wants you, and only you. Conveying romance synonymous with a best selling novel or your favorite cinematic classic, these were such exact sounds you never heard before in reality but rhetoric you dreamt of encountering and exchanging each day with a life partner. So, you think what makes you more special than any guy she has ever had? She is counting on you to be better, and she believes in you without knowing you. How do you keep this going? You enjoy the fantasy and in her mind, you believe she enjoys the story; a story that began to be written before you knew which indelible ink had been selected to start its movement.

Further, this is the woman that you thought you had no chance with, either because she was not going to be fully and perpetually attracted to every part of you, or simply because she was always going to be in relationship. You never thought she would be in range. You saw her on occasion, and when you did rarely chat with her, the outcome is that she resides more than sixteen hundred miles away. In addition, you imagine her always being in a relationship because she deserved to be treated the absolute best day after day, with respect *in love* through faith, loyalty, and sacrifice. Those small talks prior to this point with her made you believe so. Subsequently, after every one of her relationships, both in her absolute happiness and in her not-so-sure days, she inescapably articulates to you, "You're it for me…There is no one after." Oh the pressure; she places you in a position to respond. You have to respond! How does one respond? The interesting and lovely thing is that you had a validated and surviving connection with her before that moment of confession, and in every phone conversation thereafter. The chemistry builds with trading text messages, voicemails, emails, song, poetry, articles, and mailing letters in passionate envelopes of love. Again, you are falling for her tone in every dialogue, both the positive and the negative aspects. You are learning from her living moments, and you are slowly welcoming what is her history. Magically at no other time has a woman matched the exquisiteness in her eyes with the voice in her heart. You talk and you talk but there is so much physical and mental agony because she is easily over a thousand miles away. Except, this stress does not feel like the prior pain you felt in the past. You begin to slowly associate the hurt in the distance with happiness in the way she wants you, and the way you and her build connection in highly spirited conversation. So you become blinded to different time zone complications, and you focus on her and how and when she will want to be with you. Constantly, it is your ambition to want to get to know her, every edge of her, the good and the bad emotions of historic proportion. But you continue to wonder in your mind, did she start any of her prior relationships jumping the gun and saying she is "all in" and there will not be any one after? Did she start her other relationships not in the same city and with all the distance between the two? Is this a fair start? Is it too fast? You, determined and eager, want to be the man to end all guys. The obstacles are very clear, but she made a first move in confessing her crush and you feel her brave spirit. Within three weeks from the time she confessed, you take a chance and you execute a flight plan to go see her. She's welcoming you with open arms.

Oh the first feeling at the airport. Oh that brand new feeling. Now this could change you, this excursion could change her, it could either break the two of y'all a part and the realization that there is incompatible physical connection, a fantasy of misguided ramifications waiting by fate's account, or this could be something that is actually sustainable, trips and memories to build on, and a woman and a story worth believing in, regardless of an outcome.

This will be a start and a finish of finding the complete meaning behind being *in love* and putting theories to rest. This is a poetry collection, *After You, In Love Arrest*, for because of her presence with you, finally accepting both mutual love and one-sided passionate love history that came before in pursuing a relationship, and welcoming every event after her, you now know a state of Being *in love* has always carried existence deep inside a cordial and secure soul each of you possess.

So, this is my thank you. This is my goodbye. And for when her rose opens because it heard something discipline in the mist of making love, this is my hello.

IN LOVE
beautiful living moments

Weekend Made

Late at night, feeling through,
to avoid all the tears,
drinking and talking,
those two accessory wretches,
her Carpenter Eyes put light
to my photo cropped darkness.

Your body takes its shape
and moons bring our escape,
lovely woman,
you made the weekend!
Because normal days
laid too contagious;
Everyone falling apart
meant falling into
the right moments' pieces.
In every dance song left witness,
for here is a person in every line,
a life in a word,
a keepsake for all those mistakes
that made good times shared.

It's our destination
along each letter,
for there is someone's smile
to remember,
where two locked eyes signed a place,
in your young and unforgettable face.

Couldn't Let Her Stay

She says she likes me.
Couldn't I resist another man's
claimed once upon a time girl?
Am I less human, do I belong
in this different rebound of a world?
She says she likes me.
Broken and paralyzed
like my father,
addicted to shouldn't have,
and bleeding for my better half.
If cheating finds a disaster
and happy ever after,
princes versus devils,
this is what a love story is?
Not my girl on this bed,
asking what's going on in your head?
When he catches blame
like a ground consumes
piled on dead leafs,
alone on our long away from home,
do you feel my hand on your heart?

If she says she loves me,
and screams reminisce in my mind,
this is and that was I love you!
What am I suppose to do
with the two?
Contemplate trust issues
and future self-hate,
or keep kissing my neck
until I feel numb,
and it's you asking one more night
to stay, can I come?

Every girl, a bad habit retreat,
like it's my last first time,
if she hit rewind,
it's a reminder someone's past
makes me feel this alive.

Four Songs (2 Hearts, 2 Worlds)

The difference between apathy
and telepathy
is a person's voice coming to me
in a lucid dream.
And somehow your mind is glued,
when she comes to life,
late night soul entwine,
I heard four songs.
I stopped
and look at her,
my dreams, the myth of
I had never lived at all before.
All the world seemed to die,
we were the last of the seas.
I cried two rivers, one flowed
in the memory of her dream,
the other laid still as it did drain,
soaked up from all her pain.

Show me how long reality runs,
the nearest channel
to the Hudson's city?

Evil mornings drowning
for hangover water,
no answer ring,
the drink to the end of the bottle;
But questions lied in lips,
down in her talkin' ventricle
starting a new cycle.

As high as the highest peak
of every city's tower,
a heart could relay a signal
from each of our beats' scream.
Four songs, and her lil' antidote,
orchestrated a sweet vessel's
home flickerin' inseam.

Are You Right Here?

Girl who you talkin' to?
Who's taking a picture of you?
Disappear, reappear,
Are you right here?
No Facebook,
is it the same new look?
Knockin' on a concrete jungle door,
can you come out and play?
Men love their Texas hold'em,
your southern take over game
of Where's That Smile?
Is your ex askin', and
somehow he forgets to address,
a man's world shouldn't morn
in an unnoticed denial.

How do you laugh?
Do you shred a new tear?
Are you right here?
How long will you be gone?

New age questions
inspiring love when we're alone,
keeping magnetic potion,
keeping me in site,
if he returns again,
girl don't pretend,
I'm right here,
don't you disappear, no no.

Florescence

Lyrically determine
to build the perfect picture,
for one look into
the sound of your name,
reminds me
of a revolutionary change.
I don't wanna brag about the woman
I'm upon,
Tonight it's only one;
I'm more than pride
but this is what I won.
I see you laying there with your eyes
slowly at a close,
talk and talk until we meet again,
don't move your head, stay, stay,
stay on that beautiful pose.
Most times a glimpse isn't enough,
soft envelope
to the ring in a cell phone call,
my florescence
when all my darkness seems to fall.

Say, say, say
this will be greater than a moment;
Say, say, say
surreal will won't be a steal.
Dear scars, scars, scars
find light this time,
a heart can heal, heal,
heal.

Invisible Love, My Sunset Sweetheart

Woke up from the inevitable,
someone telling me
the mail doesn't move,
how am I suppose to get these letters
for you?
Sporadic recording
from a speechless face,
the queen of creative lone gestures,
with folklore poetry schemes
and unreal, the king of jesters.
Every day,
I'm struggling for a word, it's like
a peace prize chemist having another
new drug for every rare cancer.
Surrounded by a cocktail rim of a cast
in this unforgettable heart,
the pound of a sinkin' feeling
to my stomach;
When her voice meets an ear
my blood lights up
like the city skies
But who can see it glowing?

Invisible Love,
disappearing after a good night hour,
does the ocean ever go quiet,
do sweets taste as good sour?
I'd recite day by day
to have your body say,
I want you, and I need you.
Is this how I get to you?
When you're gone
all these first colors I see
halt to simply black and white,
like Avatar's Pandora
reverting back to the times
of a 1960s fedora.
As she consults a new generation
of the finds and keeps,
surviving teacher
can I be where you lay
for your cry and sleeps?

Uncanny (Dreaming Until Our World is One)

If you never heard from me again,
is there a place you would go?
That room where it all began,
you were mine,
you were mine.
The touch of a warning heartbeat,
a shadow of our sun,
that day
we were holding hands as one.
Your whispers were to me,
the world will lie,
and survivors will sing,
jealous of the peace
you found with me.

I was lost in you on the first day,
and now,
this world is beggin' for yesterday.
Pleading to a knee,
throwing eyes to the city sky,
WHY, WHY,

WHY?
Who will wonder in the tired,
tired night?
Who will stay and fight?

Love Trapped (Home By Sin)

Trapped between the door
and something to say,
he waited
for the sound of a hand's skin.
One more rejection from a woman,
the same ole God plan.

I confess, I have been broken
from an inconvenient time,
trying to capture ghosts
line by line.
Poetry locks the beating
and denying,
how this
and that will never be enough.
Love was on the other hand
of a mom and dad fight;
packing bags
and hanging up phones,
they all made me feel
like we couldn't do this alone.

Wings winded home by sin;
God said blood would be poured,
and water won't cure the thirst;
I couldn't put myself first.

Gasoline in the house
and flames in the heart;
Given and taken, losing
and holding by the finger tips,
like piano strings for veins,
those colors slowly
washed out the music in my eyes.
Angels gave me this, writing
to get you home by sin,
and love trapped in water
where the river channels begin.

Without Touch

The dialogue was in the molecules,
lips to lashes
Vibrating inside my veins,
her electric eyes hit a switch within.
Every look set
another new lightning choreography
for the dance of my heart.

Without Touch Part II

I'm staring at the portrait of your face
in my mind,
wondering if you see the same mirror
in your eyes tonight.

It's only us talkin' about the stories
of when we met;
I'm spitting out words, trying to keep
your undivided attention.
Sunkissed skin in every woman
couldn't capture
your one of a kind soul.
I don't remember
what else there's to be said,
all I can feel is an electric touch.
I could play this one way,
it's easier to look away
and not give a fuck,
but I'm flooding my one true heart
to be your everlasting friend.
In life surrounded by world's hate,
it's your voice as a means

to a patient day's mad end.
I'm asking God
and I'm asking time:
Do you have to sleep to be wanted?
Is together alone
the closest thing to happiness?
Will my head
give in to my past's forgiveness?

There are times when I see you
and you're not there;
a woman has never been able
to hold me without touch
the way you do.
Your invisible chair
symbolizing happy frustration,
crackin' and rockin' the distance
in a little boy's dream coming true.

I

I want you to hate me
because I never knew a love;
I want to create a fire
to bring back those sweats
of when I wasn't enough.
I shot ugly text messages
as protective bullets,
something I not am.
I live with the haunting stories
of a cheating father;
God can you save me
from never knowing?
How bad is it to get up there?
Can you find me an angel
through the sabotaging smoke?
I think I heard her
when she first spoke.
There are times
when I script my own war,
lying alone in a struggle
of pushing away armory so mean.
But it's really not me.

Anger from a child
with insecurity from the bricks
and trash bags of my home.
This is not me;
this is what I trade with, like
a poker dealer at a Las Vegas hotel,
he'll win and he loses,
sending home gambling stories to tell.
My mom would say girls come
and go, God stays current,
and a real patient woman will stay
if she understands your torment.
Fears are as good as dreams, I hear,
lives are as good as recognizing
the lesson from the dead, I show,
for when I want to know
new versed prophecies,
her angel will rise above
his own self-implode smoke.

I Want to Know

Staring at the minute hand
while I pretend to understand
why time passes.
All of a sudden,
I blink and you appear
like a firefly on a sweet July night.
Austin to Astoria,
she's right next to me; I'm whispering
peaceful songs about *ila*.

If your heart
had one picture frame in its room,
would it be us captured
in the lock of a set of lips?
I want to know.

At a standstill
bare foot alone in the sheets,
does your mind allow your body
to drift towards me
like a sail in search for wind?
I want to know.

If I took a dip in your skin,
would I feel the warmth of the moon
and the sun?
I want to know.

Do you pour wine
when you shred your tears?
Or do your fermented smiles shine
in the dark
with all the pain you ever felt?
I want to know.

Do you imagine two beating hearts
in the collision of love to be made?
Minute after minute,
questions slowly become
like wishful artifacts for a new world.
Cheek to cheek
after I whisper in your ear,
please kiss me
until no space in our bodies answer
the questions to my fear.

As Long As It Takes (Taking Flight)

I don't need a song to tell.
I don't need a clock's ring.
I don't need a story to unfold.
What I need is your hand to hold.
If I could no longer hear,
if the hour glass ran
its last cycle out, and if
the pieces of every scene disappeared,
I would still remember
the feeling of a first kiss.

As long as it has taken
to find one moment;
as much distance
that has filled my heart,
I find stars
which surface on my veins,
when your touch brings the skies
down upon my skin.

Weekend Made Part II

Time has a new name,
proximity a different face,
your presence,
the finishing touch of complete.
My world a step closer,
your view a bit wider,
our shared wish,
inching towards a tangible vision.

I use to think the world
about this girl, now,
her world is tongue-tied, my world.
In this apsis, too many planets
and not enough lockets;
it seems
like far from yesterday to all those
thoughts which came before,
and today capturing her every space
is all I come here to adore.

In and out the labor,
picture painted like building bricks,

her jump rope around my heart;
keep it going, please no tricks.
Some boys say
the head to toe look is overrated,
but look at what I done and found,
in search towards a mercy coast,
she set every diary precedence,
the better than any man's most.
Any machinist could never keep up
with these keys,
and those many more linguists
ran out of ink.
Babe, you brought
new life to what I use to think.
I feel every beat,
a reminiscence of your beauty
to every century's poetry.
Is this possible?
The more I contain,
the more I take a deep breath
from this hand's blood rushing
to your skin's vein.
Kiss me here,
keep my kiss waiting

when I'm not there.
Do me a favor, and keep it going,
this is what bliss is,
my heart
on my perfect victim sleeve,
what I can't help,
yearning
for a same city live discovery.

Morning Eyes

Baby brown eyes look at me,
put your hands here
right on top of my burnout skin.
Two thousand 5, 6, 7, 8, 9
and now one next to the three,
where does time go?
I say up four atriums,
then into my lips
and finding yours;
what a coincidence.
Baby, baby I will put two hearts first.
Come closer
and look
at the made weekend's sky tilt;
Dark one moment in sheets,
and instantly lit from empire life
to this starving city.

Baby brown morning eyes is it me?
Blink one time,
blink to bring the world peace
equivalent to lucky dreams;

And time
as my deepest recognized envy.
Staring at your face,
waiting for the light,
3 am, 3 more hours
and here comes tomorrow's sun.
Here I am finding you
instead of usual pillows on the floor,
secretly asleep
scared for you to hit the door.

What's the Matter?

She tells me mind over matter,
or is it the other way around
to find her in this lonely town?
I'm going crazy,
like Civil War 18th century terror and
new world ambitions.
Woman tall, woman at the bus seat,
I'd search for her at every embassy.

Baby, where
did your childhood have you play?
Baby when you grew,
where did you go
on your father's sleepless nights?

Have I hit the smoke?

It's getting harder and harder
to reminisce of our burning fire.
I want to lose us
and find me among you,

somewhere in a museum picture
when they knew peace did exist.
I don't want to fight you,
nor blame disguises
on what God gave me
in my far from poetic past.
"He's too much,
this is too much," she says,
and after all the heat
the rain will wash in,
like tears spilling
on a man's foolish days.

Where are we now,
over your favorite hill,
then down the slate of failure?

She needed relief,
and I got my sensitivity
going our own two ways,
Baby, oh Baby,
let's not go back to these days.

In This Waiting Room (ila-Heart)

Oh…*i l a*…
Something great
for as long as a moment in life;
She was perfect like a Beatles' song
I couldn't let myself remember.

If my inspiration comes
from ripped out sheets,
and what she won't let me believe,
let it be; Sing to me
how good it feels to be alone.

Time is something
in forgiving the high blood
that comes to an empty rush;
I remember nose to nose,
the only difference in you with me;
Today, nothing is left to me?
All the electric current
in her city's cable couldn't un-fill
the darkness in this room.
Why won't this seed ever bloom?

Oh...*i l a*...
Beautiful-wishful lips
and their echoes do me tender,
the cries of her touch
on my skin project,
like a reminder at each fresh moon.
This is all we were?
Movie montages in the sky,
ripped out pages;
Or unwritten lingers in the sky?
Nothing to do in heaven,
the bigger her scene time,
the more these short hands will hurt,
only such secret irreversible eyes
can make an unfair heart.

Her Precipitating Mind

Haunted by the ventilating prayers
my grandmother left;
The only true sleep I've ever received
by rosary in the hand
and an unconscious camera flash.
Fast forward to the newest of times,
in any sort of calming friend,
I've learned vulnerability
is a man's best ex.
Crazy
like a pill in a tear drop shot glass;
I dissolved so deep
I wish I could
stay drowned like gravity.
Maybe never exist
for I'm washed away
by every woman's walk,
poured in new lust *Renaissance*
writings eclipsed by lonely nights'
drunken 3 a.m. chalk.
Her academic appeal
with a body's coat

that leaves psychosis heal;
Oh how your thoughts are still
dripping in
my precipitating mind.
How they'll live endlessly
in my black crown irides,
when it's mom asking,
who brings these cries?

Generational heartbreak
like the rain leaves that stay
fall after fall, proof in the season
of a clipped dove
and wind being absent of love.
Cold sleet flooding down,
head to the ground,
staring at the shadow
of those long lost friends,
and what was never said.

"Come closer faithfully,
fear none. We're together alone."

Wide open hearts
will perfectly shatter
like a vacant window rim,
and arms will remember
the slippery hands
recapturing a bird bath home.
When they ask
for an unmasked forever,
a good-bye is his tears and her
heaven's smile way of see you later.

Whispering Droplets to Ashes in the Wondering Sky

They sing
the sun will come out tomorrow
to dry these three locked tears,
each for day excursions, and
in all those yesterdays
deciding to be colorless one.
These kidnapped clouds
child'ed the river falling,
decoded through my eyes,
alone by sinkin' sands
with her cactus rose,
the lasting vision,
on his own without a ore,
a storm mistaken him for something
that isn't buoyant any more.

Age finds its true creation
after she's gone from days.
When paper turns piezoelectricity
to her throne shaped ashes
in the wondering sky,

will he be dismissed
like whispering droplets beating
on a charming clear window side
right before the full on rain?
He's looked upon
the ill-jazz world speaking
her body glass frame as new feelings,
can never die over repetition.
Will every free man's hand replace
its beautiful harmony key axis
on these living *noches tristes*?

In Every Desperation

Dear my happiness
in every desperation,
I'm lying over the desk resolute,
crushed
at the thought of getting
a realistic expectation from you,
and continuously pretending to feel
every person that walks to me.

Am I interesting only
when love isn't fair?

Babe, did you
go for what you knew all at once?

I'm trembling warm wrapped
in thinking about my mistakes,
and what your wander-embrace
gave me in the first place.
These silly restless sins
sold the distance in my head.
Where are you now?

Did I become obsolete language?
Will passion start to count
and look to me numb?
Or everyone else
in a perfect-run change?

Dear my happiness
in every desperation,
this is no time
for the blind insecure
by a meaningless shadow.
Screaming rays
won't ever set the same, and when
the hypnotizing flock of birds call,
your name can't help but be as silent
as when the leaves cover a trail
blazing in and out the darkest fall.

All these mindful moments
come in angels
at the wake of both our eyes,
by the cycle of sophisticated days
that say one too many goodbyes,

when we begin anew by a town's
morning bright, bright mercy.

Dear my happiness
in every desperation,
face to face,
I search for you between the walls
for six inches
to let me forget,
to let me fly,
to let me believe
there's something here
amongst the *Atacama* fire and
its incurable rain.

International War Memoir

The war memoir goes out
and countries collapse;
Is it heard,
an international anthem of longing?

She wasn't from New York,
but she produced
her own Broadway blues,
named Trapped in
The Contempt of What I Mean to You.
Her eyes sketched the blockade
of skyscrapers, matched with nuclear
Texas thunderbolts in a design
of cardiac veins;
at every human's rooftop view,
blooming arms and mouths
pointed in the direction of clouds
as north as Maine's.
A thousand trips couldn't find
her type of beautiful fallen star blend
and the knowing
became a sword-blade game.

When too many spaces
can't undo the cuts,
she is the lyrics the whole world will
never gasp enough air to sing.

This, an ugly tragedy,
her laurel and his red wreath,
trailing deeper than affairs fitting
November '63 dresses
of Mrs. Kennedy.

She outdrew the paint
in each poet's hand,
these Aeschylus wounds stitched
attempt for cures
by the worst man she ever had.

Who Will Tell Me (Close Your Eyes)

Close your eyes. Mine will open
in trust of what will appear.
You're around,
but movements seem so wrong
when the beautiful waves are torn.
I'm headed in separate ways
with no one to chase me down,
only this tonic
and pearl sin in my hand.
When the flame ahead and behind
and it's gleaming instant change
come alive at the highest birth,
I'm water clinching
in everything that's done.
And who will tell me:
I shouldn't have kissed you.

I was in the dark of all this treasure.
What's gold when I can find
one too many hearts with no eyes,
in touch beyond the lies?
Spin me, take me, leave me,

this is it,
and back to a needless ready.
Did I let you control the ear too soon
from your self-made remedy?

These thousand mile tundra sounds
in my sleep seem
like premature sirens from
my past misused message in a bottle
and easy word punching throttle;
Knocked out cold
from the heaven snowslide cloud,
disposed here,
swinging like a playground child,
with some kind of cancerous cigarette
trapped in my sweltering finger tips,
feeling from the absent
more and more
less oxygen to my lips!

I didn't even know ya, took every
lonely sign from the country side,
and I found your precious pebbles
at the seabed of every ocean;

Some kind of secret to add
to this ungodly potion.
I tried to run, to hide with
diamond flashes in the heavy soil.
Shameless fantasy
short of permanent carbon ecstasy
like torn up freedom
with lung tight handle bars.

Close your eyes. Mine will open
in trust of what will appear.

If Love

Is there fairness that you have,
wooing n' stinging me from how you
and only you wanted?
Is it putting to rest
what you thought of me
for a better living written draft?
There was more than a musicless slow
dance under a summer Dallas night,
to laying down lips,
to beautiful pain whistling from
pressurized walls in the day after.
My If Love,
what would you say, if I asked,
In and out
a hundred country's cabs and inns,
can our locking hands;
can sounds of sidewalk kisses
house endless space between lungs?

Or is fairness your silence
if I find you today
and say, I still want you?

Your fulfilling thoughts
threaded and bedded a heart
which gave me chance
of what I could never become,
but everybody gives up to relive.
When you say in everything
there's a reason,
well, is there one for me wanting
to stay sewn in a dream,
never wake up
because it's as close to reality to die
in my miss and taken sleep?

Fuiste in every if love day,
suddenly,
we've become too far from there,
for fairness
is now never questioned,
from a honorary guest
at center of attraction, to searching
for my friendly congratulations
in your rarely answered digital glass.
If fairness had a disguise,
it begins at the smallest arteries

running the tissue
in your muscular soul,
then bouncing straight to mine
where I lie
towards earth's infinite cold.
This is pride, this is me, this is you,
rotating in once upon a time was
our Helios' palm nervous heat.
Now, I'm rocketship combust
to space's gravity free apsis,
wishing for one day to come home
by the dreaming memories of
inspiring love
that found something to exist.

She Is

When you meet a charming woman
and she is all the distance
replaying in your head,
it is not easy
doing those impossible things again.
What is it worth
to tell her how you feel?
For actions could never take place,
postcards, poetry, and an envelope
tracing and stamping hearts
as an only hope.
You begin to wonder if life is real?
Walking alone
seeing couples hold hands,
and a terrorizing world in ruins,
where there is one true good,
is where she is.
You can't be there,
what good is good
when it is killing him
in every body racing conversation.

Every plane in the sky
tells lonely people who they are,
waiting to come home
with deep patience;
Stay, what will stay,
She is worth all the distance.

ARREST

soulful memories detain

A Heart Once

There was a heart once imagined,
when told,
lying in the dark
of an unopened window;
a certain pair of eyes' glimpse
who could only recognize
its shadow.
For every breath,
arteries made mysteries
and broken histories;
The sound born so soft
until it got louder
as time took
to restore the same beat door,
the lonely smiles,
hypnotized them coming to adore.
There was a heart once lived
who stole,
on a neck and shoulders
which rose like redness from
newly bundled stems.

Like a reminder
in each phone morning alarm,
its garden forever grew
at every corner city street,
something trains and planes
could not escape.
Winter or May,
neighbor and stranger, it is there
rooted in justice
and for what is unfair.

This Is

I told her I wouldn't write
I'll be holding it in
but how do I cope
with the only drug I know?
I'm beggin'
like deliberate world wind
Tossin' and turnin' on shore
right before
everyone knows a hurricane to hit
It's bliss
and it's something to keep tight
like zippers
on her stunning body's dress

It's crawling out of me,
chasing the path of her scent
and how she has me
feeling this spent
I long for a wrap, a warmth,
tomorrow,
and its composing melody
I wonder if she will see

these same eyes singing,
and my tears triggering
an audience clapping?
Are they glad it's over?
Or are they waiting to pay more dues
for another silver screen
last first kiss scene?

It's taking time,
unsure boats disappearing
with only an anchor
laying awake years later
on the beach
Will the lighthouse in her thoughts
say this is home?
If I don't write, will she remember
what it means to be this alone?

I told her I would drop the pen
tie my fingers
so they couldn't direct these keys
but somehow I feel like a prisoner
if I never can release

Is it only me when her bravery says
Babe,
are you going to come with me?
I say please,
wait no seize,
or something in between
like can I stay just a bit longer
than the end of the week?

Oh this feels good, this is me,
typing and denying
what a beautiful feeling
She's a beautiful feeling
More than a moment
because This Is,
this is what happens
when a flooding body
has an unforsaken chill;
I'm here for her
as long as she wants me still

Been Feeling Your New Day

Didn't I tell you in prosody?
Volume 1; I'm depleting intimacy,
I'm learning the trade,
haven't made a commitment
in half of this decade
I only need to learn,
recover through ignorance
So who knows what This Is?
Been feeling only your next move
Who can blame me?
All I get to feel is the weekend,
been feeling the craft in Oh God,
Babe when will it end?
In and out you,
is our skin really like this here;
Where are you?
On a scale from 1 to 10,
this heaven has been drizzling,
satisfying
off any measures of the Richter
magnitude

Don't look down on my swirling
tongue madness, this is greater
than what is the becoming you
So let me
continue to kiss your fountain
Keep bringing me your way,
the way like your song from Ariana
Oh but This Is,
the one, and only *ila*...

I could care how men will dare,
but who will come
when they've already been there?
Isn't life about what's new
and what will struggle to change?
I hang up the phone,
and I wonder why I spoke
I don't mean to guilt trip you
Life is a delayed wicked flight;
It's how two healing curved wounds
sleep for ending-night
I'm trying to avoid replay in a bird
releasing the last feather;

'Til the wait is over to watch you fly
on your own
regardless of immense weather
You're alone, I'm alone,
it's a next best thing
I don't know everything
when you are everything
All I got is prescriptions to prove,
what push comes to shove,
and what remedy
will never be enough
Can't I simply feel,
what is to want more?

Zen, I need *Zen*,
stop what is the past
has made me pretend
This is now, that was then,
I could love you only for one day,
like you for years but all I ask
is for one meditating moment,
no pressure, no words,
no lust,
no one is righteous,

when has merry-making
never been jealous?

Motives will be lost
in highest of mountains
when I've ascended
through what everyone has shared
Most people feen
to relive those times,
what is provided to a foreign man
What I live is girl
put here in your work pages when
we archive in this go around,
with what you need, who is he?
I know I've been rewarded
with receiving a goddess in you
In my real dreams, I'm living bless,
sometimes unjust,
often I ask what is this about?
I see you, call each other's name
with a body touching shout
How professional,
how sacred

you always will be to me
To not ask for new love, new pain,
and renewed happiness
is always in the latest future,
nothing I, you,
can't discover to figure

Give me a numbing lesson;
Give me honest voice
I'll try to uncover a different mind
Go live your own choice
There will forever be
morning water to wash away,
instantly, what you
can no longer hear a body say;
And in pure assurance,
in spilt-life missions,
there will be some sealing reason
for us to talk in your new day

Run Dry Trust

She says I don't need anybody else
or maybe I'll go back
to what I had before
or fast forward again,
to paperbacks
for standing a chance, beggin'
What's next, Ms. Friendliness?
Tell me what's next?
Used up charming boy consumed
by thunder struck sex,
love to lust?

Stop your romance bitchin' boy,
the sweetness has run dry!

Since I've been sixteen
last thing I remember
is the majority,
the sound of enlighten room strings
like pianos and violins
in the background of a kiss when
sleet has skid thru the abandon sheet

until a full on stop!

Best thing I never had
What was dancing
was slipping all this time,
landing face down
one time blue,
seven times beautifully
naked mirror red
and in-between when we leave
secret bruising frames here

Executed Temptation

I know what it was
in the mist of what money spent
Receipts won't be creditably read
Our animal bass in the backdrop,
no new neighbors going to hear
the grinding in love
Moment so color blinded to feast
and how the sun seems
to find the same bedlam rest
Up all night, certified pills sold in
the polite form of baby,
pick up your shit, you have to leave
early in the morning

He won't know,
permanence is never meant to stay
She'll hear from her *ila* man
and all the other girls
in leftover sweat dance
and what I already
surrendered to her in advance

This is going to define me
The difference between
a want and a need
like stitches, or staples
for a deep bleed
I saw these similar times before
Her sit down at the lounge,
same look in her eyes;
What am I doing
in duping this boy?
I don't belong here
Her big city dark lights blend
with his staring eyes
Looking like missed cabs
and a dollar
misleading full wallets' escape;
Flying like it's her usual business,
check in and check out,
the same metaphor for how
she fucks to say
she holds one true love

Cable car in the clouds,
be ready for this,

stay ready for the lift off
and the coming downs
It's not just a me sin
Turn around let's do it like this
Test run,
because tomorrow we will be done
No true chance,
manipulating the odds
like casino days on the card deck
Babe, come over here,
start with my fragile part of you go
with this wanted neck
Right now
this is simply executed temptation
Not with you,
I can't give you a relation
You're not ample
for a working exclusive,
but take this manipulation
All we have is right now
tomorrow
you're going to ask me how
And I don't have time for this

She'll leave you in a circle
like puff, puff pass
game of gateway drug
This is detox cut, cut an organ
left in a blizzard
Say trust, trust, oh fuck oh fuck!
This feeling is as told
in the way she uses
vapor snow mud to be sold

The Numbers

Bus passes
like every man who gave affection
Into her taunting professional
selfish love victim attention;
A darkness kindle,
her personalities dismantle
They hate me
in every corner of the alley
Every girl fuck for every brick
laid on these buildings

I'm about to show them love
Walls collapsing one by one,
the air of shaking heads,
here I come
Mix a little tramadol
to secure the weight of holding
two beautiful spines
Chimay in an empty liter
covered by a napkin in the trash
They can't know

I'm here at her soon disowned
convenience to recognize how quiet
she will keep this longing disguise

Dirty beds unfold to cemeteries,
I think I want to die here
Army full of ties
detach from a lethal cross
Demons released, shackle screams,
barbed wire stretched to the teeth
and it's now or never lips
opening up
Come near this umbrella, but
refrain new pity of who,
what won't be given from me

Love me baby,
Love me along the road
when I don't count
melting in the dead grass soil,
until I explode

Baby, You Coming?

Perfectly undone angelic breasts,
left to right my hands,
unknowingly feeling peaks
to my demise
over undiscovered atmospheres,
digging to find her sternum,
hmmmmms, and a compass
sealed ahead of an atrium
Ayy, body so timeless, a lion saint
staying young like Brigham
But this is every woman
rattling my fibers,
roaring fanatically
like a sold out stadium

Baby, you coming?

Twisting vine knots
quicker than her arch drops
There goes the tights,
goose bumps all the way down
and so smooth her legs,

like fresh era whiskey mixed cold
in cubes
imported from Antarctica flights

Baby, you coming?

Showering in sentiment soaps
Oh, her centicurves emergin'
and splittin' torso finer
than runway shows

Oh beggin', hatin' comes in the
memory of what shouldn't exist
One imaginary night of true life,
two ardor full weekends more,
and it comes to this
Playing with suspicious minds,
love all shook up and
another number on the revolution
There it goes, Elvis' guitar rolls
Hair turning and breathing blue
Expectations like
red jail slam doors firing at once
Are we drunk off happy sweat?

Or sober in lonely
for a routine touch?

Shattering and repaving
loaned out trust
It approaches every morning
like her full time job
Slow asymmetry in that sun
And killing humiliation pain
with crack of ousted light at night
But leaving juicy reminders by AM
like left out dryin' dinner dish cups

Baby, you coming?

Teach Me

Up
then
Down the staircase
again
Examining, bit
by bit her footsteps, tap with
graceboard splints,
physique as gorgeous front to back
that remains in these imprints

I'm right here
You don't have to smell the roses
It's okay to enjoy flattering
when you say to yourself
it's okay to see the fault
in a waiting to break free crystal jar
Come out to play,
it's more than a shade of coral
when the lights in the room
are beginning to turn on
Here doesn't have to begin
pushing me away

and never knowing again
one sweet day
You remember that 26th day
There is our silence
with slippery echoes
My confidence will hit
every fiber of your body's competition
in different brand new
connection's ambition
So for everything you believe
outside your profession
Teach me how to love
Teach me to find peace
Oh tell me what's good with mercy
of nothing more to be said
Teach me what will be enough
When my hands get weary
and my body knows the same
Teach me to dream change
Bring love to life
In a moment
that won't come too soon
Teach me the sense of evaporation
Let me lose, let me find

What will we do
when you is me and me is you?
Teach me what will be true

We will be so technical
Then so physical
Should I press send?
Should I be wasted?
Should I be criminal?
Okay,
so you're frustrated and the notes in
my love seem like madness
but what's heard when
there are no written scripts from
you to me to have clemency a listen

Into

When the leaving came
he didn't hurt you
But all you seem to do
is running into
the hurt of someone who loves you

Out the airport, your chest is lit
In the sheets, it won't stop blinking
Am I here? I can feel your heart
It's talking
and asking me questions
So I speak in return
Hidden pain is happy
when you allow the feeling to burn

In the beholder,
what is there that lies?
Baby, Baby, oh Babe!
Run, run into me
with what is newly feared
I don't want the knowing,
beyond reality,

I want dreams to be heard
Is there a God in this room?
Oh God!
Where will her rain remain?

When the leaving came
he didn't hurt you
But all you seem to do
is running into
the hurt of someone who loves you

Do you ever put on a smile
in the dark wishing to glance at him?
Right before he smiles,
you close your eyes
and enjoy what's inside you
All of those
who been running freedom in you
But can you differentiate the one,
the one loving you,
to secure more than fuckin' you,
like it won't ever be temporarily
a pleasure city boy friend routine

Who will tell you who you are
in the ugly,
in your most professing ideas
by the way of being so mean?

There was a day and time
at the longing table,
waiting for last flame
in a wick of a candle
Where I expose those who could
never make a love like this
Where I use to sit back,
write what came before you
like the unraveling Juliet strings
of a love suicide rhyme
Soon autumn arrived
believing chances existed
like these left over spring waters
coming from skyscrapers
and street side puddles

When the leaving came
he didn't hurt you
But all you seem to do

is running into
the hurt of someone who loves you

Holding hands in love 'til
we evolve to atomic braille
You walk ahead,
fugitive fused with wind,
and every reflecting subway sign
became a souvenir
for my solitary hope,
stuck in a real place
to imagine you and I
connecting
such guilty sweet avenue lines

Maybe, oh hey!
I'll find your ever seen spark,
in any amount of distance
And for each time they all do
like I do,
I'll think
of an overprotected heaven's gate,
you running to break into

For the Last Time (If Love Doesn't Care)

Yo like me back
like this is some Facebook crap
Baby,
oh she's worth more than that
Maybe he's the first poet
to come out,
straight new haven gay, no,
not that sexual orientated desire;
Producing vivid word portrait,
highly spirited,
when her words become limited
Who is she
when everything she wants,
an illusion of need is on her lap,
unclothed,
and written in the next book
she began to barely open?
But maybe being open
is done with an era ago,
slow mind strip with the lights off
and soul lift to pink clouds
When she stood up

on that last date to find first love;
the future on her own,
leading direction
in the same perfect circle
Oh so close to giving up,
there's no such thing
as just the two,
this world is an unbreakable,
endless popsicle
Tasting this and flavor dressing
but never getting
to the very center of her heart,
Her United Center
like being in the wind chill Chicago

Morning Eyes, make up gone,
nude, and full of thought
For the last time can he foray again
'til the past of love ones comes
to this future he wants to call home
Did she plan to only fuck,
rip out his skin
to see the shape of his angry heart?
She's worth more than that

by bull's-eye in the touch
of both of their eyes as they talk
'til she feels something to prone to
like the foot in her walk before
she holds his hand and they leave for
another night take off

Was he a mistake?
Or everything she needed to kidnap
her own spirit of being safe alone?
Oh! She will attack
without regard for consequence
Bullying classroom behavior is
like her sexual prowl chance loom
For that first person who cut
and ran away with the glue,
look how confused collage dreams
have If Love doesn't care too

Time Zone, Sleeping Alone

Don't get it twisted,
thanks for the hurt, the lesson
He's grown up
in and out the wrong beds
and those he made think
of how her body will impress
It's a wild guess,
we are one in that same body,
same heart,
but different projected face

She can push away *Karma*
and run with her chamber-trapped
thing between lungs
For now, he's become out of control,
attached to the map, cursing, and
pulling more until he's decomposed
He is laying still
The furthest from discipline
and what won't let her win
because no girl he took
has ever been his

Trust is a broken security lock,
closed without a code
What happen to his combination?
Different time zone has him spitting
this mask of words
as if they were in a cell bound
for one escaping to find
patience on their own

Where is she now?
Oh where is she now?
New city found sparks,
left on the rebound,
or in her own struggle
with camouflage fuck mes
and let's cuddle?

There will always be new music
and some kind of new technology
to keep her unnoticeably
attached
to that very first boy she loved
Or those in-between
who can't be enough

Some Kind of Queen

Is there denial,
embrace in the way
she slips into classy heels,
a fashion constructed bridge to him?
He is telling her too,
wait to walk over the breaking boards
Because he felt it, lived it
He knows what makes people
go around;
the lead talk of that new town

He flirted fortune
with too many dancers
and disappeared young cheerleaders,
too many secrets
and not enough answers
He should have said
he saw her all along
on the medieval court
like she was some kind of queen
While still she is being flattered
by the boy of her dream,

who wasn't ever going to be king
Guinevere, amid pretty boys and
a man, will say like me back
But
who will have
the only time of the day
that means just as much as when
we're busy in profession neglectin'
but giving equal devotion back?

Too happy to recognize happiness
Feels so good alone
As much as we want somebody
endlessly, we're twerkin' weekly on
technology keys discreetly
sublimely asking,
telling him do you still want me?

Why does it take so long
to forever let in
one weekend passing moment?
When he's immutable sky
she refuses the star,
and so many times

shooting fidelity she will deny
Come down, come down,
calm down
She looks to him
and him
to stay in connect
like the air she breathes
Like the other duchesses
who came before, so much energy
she uses from those boys entering
her inner earth field of dreams,
what career leaves,
and for other hunger moments
in shadow language
for what permanent crop she retrieves

My Window and I

There wasn't much outside,
but a pure glow
I swear I saw her
beneath the curb cement,
just my window and I
with the blinds bent,
it was around the same time
that I went
Curtains always waiting
innocently undone,
and I look to the bed laid
without movement
As I made my shameless pace
back and forth,
only the moon
could keep the wonder alive,
because it's the last dotted light
I remember
in her beautiful misplaced darkness

We made no ceiling, to be visible
from any whistle in the failing sky

When we vanished,
I would stay,
and every time I say,
"If you ever come again,
you will be these dusty strings
holding my dreamcatcher,
untouchable,
remaining up so high"

You, You, You Moment

I use to believe in time and a state
But you,
you grabbed me at the edge,
at the edge
Here we go,
diving in matrimony vines
of immortal reflection
No more temptations,
an unfinished exception

I stand here, talking swirls down,
obsolete
But I feel no turbulence
in our ocean starting to hit the sand
on these four happy feet
Up higher,
filling each space
to where nothing exist
Baby don't,
don't cry to a crack of laughter
And please,

I promise no little woman's heart
could smile any harder
Like a child who figures out
there's light after here comes now
sweet, sweet cradle nighttime
You're here, I'm here
No need for a lullaby played softer

Spinning faster,
taking off towards every place
You take me to moneyless work
from there, you, you,
you steal me in this
I want be where you are presence
To a never seen planetless future
my, my,
my endless hanging sky up, up allure!

Sorry It's Cold in Invisible Arms

She said, sorry I had to go
There wasn't much to be there
I could see it in the troubling wind
behind that beginning stretch
in the rest of a life shape
unfolding in brown eyes
and pouring fabric partake

In chills
he stumbled upon a wildflower
So he hung on tight to the stems,
staring at yellow like save me
with your irreversible umbrella face!
And any position he stands
is a mirror glass floating out to sea
on broken pieces
of this amazing shadow quake,
trapped
in her invisible arms

He said sorry
for knocking myself silly
and wondering so many times
wow him, me and him, really?
Those unsure rude bursts
and an in-between,
our origami dream
They called it a stateless message
for endless ivies that were knotted
left in one-sided joy's hanging cut

It didn't last longer
than those that always seemed to find
unforgivable affection on the last try
Maybe the curing gold
ran through a vessel all along
And glitter was reborn inside
beyond the need for a make up song

Two body skins collapse
will always be louder
than the sound of water
when 7 billion dive in
for the same rescue me search splash

And all those come and go quicker
than her restful woman's eye
projecting a bonfire bloody boy's ash

She said sorry I wasn't meant to stay
His reply,
I can leave these thoughts
in silent vibrating vein form,
like your orchestrated symphony
rattling crave
Pounding deeper and deeper
blood flowing
fresher in skeletal cliffs,
counting to jump
with the end of those
who thought they could follow
a flame you killed in me

What's left to recapture
this human nature ready to die
into what I was given,
Too far ice-sculpted with crazy
and I can't breathe above the abuse
your soul pastels seem to leave

Remember when you see
the fading light in island sun
as it cuts down,
I'm being pumped back to life
waiting for my lips to brace
for an endless freeze
And I'm sorry too, to move through
living by my deserted shivers
coming at your finger tips
of flawless ease

Sweeping Feet

She woke up my eyes
making a forever young and old
the burn melting each cold
On grown man music
what women left like debris
gave them my time
until she changed me

I learned sweeping feet
when the skies are low
and Sundays come to watch her go

I wondered
if she would remember
my name,
mysterious sunsets,
the flight,
Oh Baby, kiss me now,
and how long tonight?

Keeping chemicals through phone,
she instilled classic like buying
brand new '60s vinyls at the store
no download, no stream,
but she brought falls like Niagara
beyond control,
she felt B.C. like Cleopatra
filling every cessation secretly,
angrily, deeply
My Queen of lady dynasty

Every Memory

Love comes as fast as time
She's not that far behind
Shot down from flight to flight
Hands in bloody slings,
contagious mind over matter
Smiles looking
like no happy ever after
Yesterday's darkest cold
disguised in a waiting room
No one mutually around,
scratches on the floor,
curtains in empty corridor
Sunk by my own veins
Slow, slow Jackson bed potion,
then no dance motion
You and me
You and me
Her last morning brown eyes
became
new world dialogue realize

24 hours a day, 362
I stop one time, remind myself
I wasn't thinking about you
Babe, really it's you
I can't feel this
seconds from pill delay
Mercy, take
More than memory away

Head to toe,
between, inner and out
hip to hip ratio,
there left shelves of words
for my linguist I adore you code
She knew her affect
waving mirror cut unfathomed glass,
full of fire once,
then weekend cashed
Literary dreams skinning seams
from a limited start
to endless wakes
give chance at heart

Sleep, sleep jungle streets
Wait for arrival
by colliding speakeasies
bringing those passenger signs
Like poetry poured into decagon cups
Wise letters shooting
in parachuteless drop
Ayy, I couldn't keep up
She wasn't going to let me
Let me be enough
At every rise to occasion left
all the men that been through
The taste ended each third night
Living with a stranger in you

24 hours a day, 362
I stop one time, remind myself
I wasn't thinking about you
Really it's you
I can't feel this
seconds from pill delay
Mercy, take
More than memory away

My excursion, you,
oh sweet *Chilean* disaster
like flippin' then reinventin'
every *Neruda contigo* latitude
Tangled butterflies floating up,
chest bloodstream quivering harder
For *Mi Corazon*
My Never Could Be Alone
She welcomed me
to Latin Capulet roulette
Practice dose so far from perfect
Rehearsal brought a man to his knees
All the world's possibility in grief
Learning to lose found
body sutures releasing creativity
So this is what is left of me,
pieces chipping a turned stone
shadow by human suffocating light
My gray kiss me goodnight
revitalized every perch in sight

I was going to search for her again
again,
and someone like her again

24 hours a day, 362
I stop one time, remind myself
I wasn't thinking about you
Really it's you
I can't feel this
seconds from pill delay
Mercy, take
More than memory away

In Love Arrest

i...l...a...
A dream begins
in love arrest
the call, the fall, the mind, the sex
Never will it be enough,
handcuff the wrong,
kick me down, pass me along
Some professional,
some irrational,
some full of disrespect
Forgive them, but who can forget?
i...l...a, in love arrest
in love arrest
in love arrest

in love, I rest

Timetraveler

Timetraveler
will you welcome me?
Not too far behind
Not too far ahead
to each in their mind
I come here quick
Unarmed, unleashed for peace

Timetraveler
do you know where we sin?
Forgive for they found
no way to cry
Water has been sucked
from what is left of their eyes
Wells as souls, drunk
making love to strangers,
breathing empty 'til blood turns dark
Laughter coming out that same alley
Everyone at standstill,
touches steal,
but nothing expressed verbally

Timetraveler
do you ever want to stop?
Give advice for the next
Cure our self-inflected appetite
and destroy potions
Find more smooth sails
on clear blue oceans

Timetraveler
where is your home?
It's getting late,
can you come back?
Again in love, or is this
an over-ran one-too-many date?

I'll reach out again
when pain is so deep
and happiness puts
your children to sleep
Don't any one worry
Past is a foundation
for all of beautiful creation
When your future calls, say yes
Say you believe

I'll leave you a road
for what together
torture and tranquil
we're here to handle,
every morning
that sun
is our special forgiveness candle

Poems Don't Stop

Don't stop. Keep imagining
where you will go
and who will be there.
Don't give up on a paradise
you have created.

There are some
who grab your hand and others
who will stare from a distance.

It will not be easy.
Hate will live on and no force
strong enough to have it stop.
Poison will sink
before you have had a taste.
The garden you seek
is full of illuminating colors
and don't let any liquid
keep you drowning
to reach that green.
Voices will tell you to give up
and there will be echoes of decay

like a suffocating school hallway.
You cannot be angry.
Anger weighs your body
where you can't move.
Remove that anchor; although you
will need it from time to time,
free your movement,
ride those waves guiding atonement.

Swim if your boat collapses.
We cannot stop searching.
Your blood will thump, thump,
at your skin asking for revival.
Live with this skin
and connect it with others
who share a same path.
Dark or light, wrinkled or fresh,
there is a message concealed
in each eye that fights.

Don't talk, simply listen
to every harmony language
of the silent body.

It's one of a kind,
built from beach night's injecting sand
into elegant spurs
of clasping woman and man.

Your Deepest

I'm sorry I tried to embrace
your deepest insecurities
as becoming mine too.
Love is together,
not alone.
One day,
I will thank you
for giving up on me,
and releasing love so free.
Somewhere
our spirits
do forever speak.
"We were greater than the moments."

Unrecoverable

disposed of
my soul

If my soul
bled by stars,
there is a meteor storm
welcoming
heaven and hell as one.

If I had one power,
I would eliminate the word "was"
so every human will say,
"Love IS there."

Not a Poem but a Witness

Look around you
and see if you can witness
a moment outside your body,
but deep inside the parameters
of your heart's temper.

Fully present
is how people are given new life
in a minute's flash.
That is a powerful spiritual Being
we have, which collectively
carries our journey.
Beyond distance, beyond time,
you and I
have a deeper inner space
we contribute to the world
through each other.
Before we knew
who one another were, are,
fate remained in existence
waiting by birth to imaginings
for us to share.

Talks, touches,
divine executed presence
brought it to physical reality.
This world,
as big as it is,
we found two spirits,
two spheres,
connecting,
continuing,
for we attested to planets
in every second,
there is a ceaseless calm
humans can spring.

Endgame

Call it possessive or aggressive
for a cheap syringe
Her puppet play
with a man's veins
Her kisses like pawns
moved to a full blood cardboard box
In game of chess
And furiously into this chest

I breathe you
I taste you

Cuts

When all the world's roses first bloom
and they are cut to be given
in the spring,
remember one thing:
For each dying petal will begin,
in their silence,
there lies my heart peeling
inch
by inch,
wishing, waiting
for if I ever find you again.

Of Will's Keeper

O Ms. Echosmith,
O Ms. Cutson

My Captain! Of wind Will sail
Destiny of tippin' tongues
Keeper of physics
Law of love, she gives?
Will of love, I have
Will of law,
Will you love me?

O Ms. Collaborate,
O Ms. Regenerate

Preying crush,
under Armageddon melanin;
Fluttering together the hottest
like new bang theory
My Mastermind! Of darkest energy

Now I knew I lost her -
Not that she was gone -
But Remoteness travelled
On her Face and Tongue.

- Emily Dickinson